Weaver in the Sluices

You know me by my towpaths
My echoes strewn with brine
The way I carry narrowboats
And water gypsy time

You fashion me with locks
And send me shunting north
A weaver in the sluices
With a shadow standing forth

Weaver in the Sluices

selected poems by
Daniel Staniforth

SKYLIGHT
PRESS

First published in Great Britain by Skylight Press,
210 Brooklyn Road, Cheltenham, Glos GL51 8EA

Designed and typeset by Rebsie Fairholm
Printed and bound in Great Britain

www.skylightpress.co.uk

ISBN 978-1-908011-08-4

Contents

Acknowledgements	8
Intro	11
Unretainable Past	12
Amidst the Crooked Ray	13
The Touch of Parched Lips	14
A Fear of Autumn	15
Where Herb and Homo Reach	16
Trance	17
Youth at Sundown	18
The Heresy of Impetus	19
Life – A Grave-robber's Feast	20
The Penultimate Smile	21
Lamentations of a Thought Untold	22
The Rusty Iron Welcome	23
Destined	24
Half-dead, Wholly Damned	25
Journey to Event	26
She Sketches the Rose	27
Self Propagation	28
Agile Laziness	29
Skinfliction	30
Sight-Sea	31
Mirror of Mud	32
Screen Door	33
Disciple Dare	34
Double Negative	35
21st Century David	36
Tears of the Drowning Man	37
Shadow of the Scythe	38
The Giggle – A Life	39
Gorge of Senses	40
Ruin	41
The Forest Kiln	42
Protholic	43
Carriage Car	44

In a Church of Flaunting Ghosts   45
Autopsy   46
Needling the Priest   47
Unconsigned   48
Face of the Deep   49
Disappear   50
Apparition?   51
Shafted   52
Inlet Drift   53
The Deep   54
Primordial   55
Autumnal   56
Inhumanation   58
Ice Flower   59
Babbla   60
Sylvan Forest   61
He Grew Bogus   62
The Pretender   63
MEmorial   64
Mystical Eyes   65
Staggering Space   66
Langue Secrète   68
Orchan   69
Fireworks at Makr al-Deeb   70
The Scream   74
Desire   75
Tribal Voids   76
Depointed   77
Xenomarket   78
Trappist   79
Ubar   80
Albion Twine   81
Sudden Poetry Corner   82
Spume to Illume   83
Prayer to the Veiled One   84
Fabula   86
We evil   87
Mooted Mute   88

In the Valley of the Meuse	89
Boethus	90
Papaver Rhoeas	91
Song of the Cephalon	92
Offsprung	93
Escondig	94
Armageddon Lust	95
Death-grip Love	96
The Final Dowry	97
Marlais	98
Somnium Mihi Verus	99
The Aeolian Catch	100
ωμέγα	102
To the Luna Sensitives	103
Luminosity	104
The Marketable Seer	105
Pastorelle	106
A/V	108
Moon Couplets	109
Wood Nymph	110
Graven	111
Phantasy	112
Mary's Lake	113
Hydropaddle	114
Propelle	115
Epon)a	116
uilleann	117
Pitiless	118
Pep Tide	119
Oneiroi Open House	120
Tetrapodular Assent	121
Ascent	122
Folly	123
Genea	124
About the Author	125

Acknowledgements

The poems contained in the volume span a number of years with the latter half being written between 2008 and 2010. I would like to thank *Rogue Poetry Review*, *The Houston Literary Review*, and *Monkey Puzzle* for featuring poems in their journals. Audio soundscape versions have also appeared in *Trickhouse*, *InStereoPress*, *Not Enough Night*, and on my *Poetscapes* page. Song versions for various poems can be found on my three Luna Trick CDs (*Total Submersion*, *Hoar Frost Sheen*, and *Prophetic Guesses*), Dream nth CD *(Moonbather's Glory)*, and on forthcoming recordings by Luna Trick, Alchymical Muse, and Rebsie Fairholm.

See www.flowforth.com for more information.

Many thanks to my family, to those I love, and to the many that have inspired and encouraged me along the way.

"How have you left the ancient love
 That bards of old enjoy'd in you!
 The languid strings do scarcely move!
 The notes are forc'd, the notes are few"

— William Blake

"O! for a muse of fire, that would ascend
 The brightest heaven of invention"

— William Shakespeare

Intro

Always introspection
Vulgar vines of hindsight
Creeping innards
Tracks between the shells
Bulbs of forethought
Shooting bloodward

Unretainable Past

Corridors of diminished time
Enslave an active memory
Pictures circulate an interior room
Irritated by their vagueness

Completion so imperfect
Perfection so incomplete

The paradoxical remedy
Neither soothes soreness of heart
Nor relieves tension of mind
Never to return
Never to retrace
Only to retract
In the near blank corners of recollection

Amidst the Crooked Ray

Colours collide in deep opaque
    Ornate lights willingly fuse
Prism overloads the spectrum
    Jaded glass on a distant shelf

Crystal show for inquisitive people
    Transient sparkles travel freely
Spurned in sticky public hands
    Desecrated in unknown homes

Ignorant scoff – mind too easily spent
    Ornament for impulsive wealth
Stone once honed by the elements
    Wasted on plush unnatural velvet

The Touch of Parched Lips

Balancing on the edge of dreaming
Reality sets with the russet sun
As muffled voices ebb menacingly
From distant and unknown tables

Such spacious time I numbly muse
Drifting over still-born words
Searching for expensive thought
To appease the vanity within

The room bellows its strange expanse
The walls stained in shallow travel
A thought spent is a thought earned
In this womb of city silence

I look for a silver goblet
To toss against this inner thirst
But all I see is silver shadows
That only quench a thirst gone by

I betray the day that bears this spite
Look to a day of future birth
When the cracked lips of time renew their softness
And wake me from this death-cold sleep

A Fear of Autumn

On time's command
    I fall with the dead leaves
Fluttering and cowering
    toward the looming grass
Then I lie wasting
    decaying on a bed of life
Shrivelling madly
    as growth swells all around
I become tangle
    in the surge of another
His limbs frolicking for the sky
    mine splintering in death
Begrudgingly I crack with heat
    segment into tiny pieces
Bits of once vivid being
    strewn at the mercy of the breeze
I become scattered
    tiny particles of anonymous dust
Spanning miles
    without sense nor direction
Some inert sense of salvation
    collects me to the tree
Clinging to the gnarled frame
    with rationed strength
Relishing the sun's westward arc
    one more time
Til the servants of time
    tear me again

Where Herb and Homo Reach

When silence vexes its unconstraint
Young vagabonds await a mending pride
Stillness yearns a healthy jolt
And placid eyes are bruised transfixed
The vapoured soul scarce collects its dew
The goblet snatched by angered heat
In rallying, the night's forged impress
To move and garb the silhouettes

Nature's clients, all wounds dressed
Dance there with re-admonished power
All fugitive and free of blood
Yet glean the mercy of the globe
It's as if all were a single strand
An aged hand would loosely knit
But blood will spill, for all a stitch
And stain the woven callous knees

Await young piratical night
To yield – unspending – in the stillness
With solar tyrants in absentia
Young strand repair your severance
Yet noiseless with nocturnal chaos
And all limbs donor to the loom
Would spin a shoot to lofty height
And weightless, kiss the shyest god

Trance

Usurper of monotony
   Sweet heir of delirium
      Flexing youth unconstrained
        In shapeless colours
          Behind the veil of dormant eyes

Youth at Sundown

Insipid vainglorious time
    Ever diminishing
Whilst disquieting diminuendos of life
    Rage mute
Perplexing echoes on man's soul

Scarce the sun parades its newborn brilliance
It plunges agonisingly
    the oceans to boil

Pretentious copious man
    imitation of light unbreathed
Trading photons for infectious lumps of black revere
That we
    our vagrant selves
        should disperse
As elements segmented
    rent by tyrant winds

The Heresy of Impetus

That doubt (emphatic) lies down
The murder of a premise withstood

      To all
Soft fragrant light would manipulate
        With all
To tell of life ill-used

Take a stick and smash the platter
That epitaph sulking silent on the walls
Breed havoc with the grain of its words
Diminish its intent to a frown

Take a rock and ground the shrine
        That impiety
Grabbing shadows in the soul
        Of its edifice
        Reduce to a fossil
That future may calculate its ailing worth

Life - A Grave-Robbers Feast

A small diffusing light
Encumbering the brain with frolic
Out-dated flowers fashion graves
As symbiotic pleasure nuances

Yet light will smite the stone
Beneath all its vegetation
With splintering rays of truth
The bellows breathe cold peace

Death unshelled
Anonymity stolen
Life poaches significance for game
Even the sun threatens occupation
Like fire-dissolving rain

Yet dance on we
Lethargic gardeners of this celibate soil
Casting bouquets like bundled wreaths
On garlands of dismay

Still galloping light
Transfused with night
Our leather notions fraying
Spin the needle through the cloth
Our self-fabricated clay

Live on fancy
Feast on greed
Sensation pierces our opaque greys
Tempts the colours from the spectrum
Uniting nature with its mad intent

The Penultimate Smile

Fat on lip
The width of a star
The accursed smile
Ostracizes once more
Stretching
Mutating
With foreboding teeth
Capped with venom and lust
Bite into desire
Feast from the source
A dog at another king's ankle
Ripping and gnawing
Into the substance
Which of itself
Leaves no heir

Lamentations of a Thought Untold

Live-in self-abandon
Pale nemesis of aspirations
Shackled to dream meanders
Deep eternal fires
Freezing at the surface

Already imprisoned
Unransomed spirit in the fleshy cage
A feeling
Sharp and bloody
Yet exhausting
Vital self-enclosure

Oh to stab a way out
Tear through tissue
For a solitary breath
To burst the vacuum
And climb the icy staircase to death

The Rusty Iron Welcome

Life
As a gate
Hinges on a borrowed smile
Whines a greeting sadly loaned
Pierces the garden with a promise of peace
Then swings reversed
with a beckoning grin
And points to a door
Painted shut

Destined

Whimsical
Leaves
Revolving doors
In wind
Mechanical float
Bearing down on earth
Awkward resilience
Piercing the night
The crack of a fickle limb

Half-dead, Wholly Damned

Black-eyed reminiscence
      Groping still
Pains elocution to its breathing sigh
Sends exhaled pleas
      Dancing upwards

Rolled-globes
      Swollen beyond all carriage
Given of effort
      A formidable thief
Excises last pleas to occupancy

The final fruit of misery
      Paralytic
Its succulent burst under the tongue
Brings wishes
      To final last collapse

Journey to Event

Abandon self
Grope beyond nothing to the empty core
Plot spacious travel
Beyond the chimes of muted bells

They fall at leisure
As feathers on guided wind
Colliding with self
And sky eclipsed beyond

Buttress the fictional soul
Spin – wheel-top – spin
Circular furrow to pleasure's end
Mark balance pointedly
Fling the ellipse round
Centrifugal fuse
Coloured demand

She Sketches the Rose

Ever rueful
The blood-red knot
Shimmers on its narrow needle
Smiling pungence
It sweats its rouge-naked glory
And beckons all to damp velvet folds

How softly
It envelops itself
Each petal swaddling the soul

How brutally
Its thorny stand
Enamoured like the Stegosaurus tail

Nature's most amorous of damsels
Chastity of force
The Serape knight defends
Then imprisons
To parade untarnished glory
Until age beheads the withered jewel

And how readily she bears her sacrifice
The fatal wound her only womb

Self Propagation

When fruition comes to the self
It comes in small red clusters
        Ruby knots
Hard impenetrable bulbs
Newly formed on a twisted tree
        But only time ripens
Maturity alone sweetens
And softens these virginal forms
This is where I stand
In the first metabolic phase
Red
        hard
                sour
Yet threatening a soft glow

The waiting cannot hospitalise my intent
Only the wanting

Agile Laziness

It plunders the body
Quickens the mind
Swims on the circumference of the skin
And heats the blood with friction

It is achievable by choice
Unavoidable by chance
Distorts everything with its shadowy unconcern
And spins its frenzied nothingness into shape

Landlocked by flesh
Thwarted by spiritual convalescence
Cased-in as an oyster
Writhing in a prison shell

Truth lacks youth
An eternal age of vapid repugnance
A revolving door to rampant normality
Spin madly
Anaesthetised by centrifugal force

Then smooth out the jellied innards
With some remote commiseration
Noise is personal
To each it bears a treacherous visitation

To the impotent ear – it is silence dressed up
To the austere – it is silence coloured in

Skinfliction

Take me out of sensitivity
Damn my touch and self-pleasing feel
Let me be without bloated weight and meddling reason
Eclipse my light and paint my dark

Let me breathe rivers and sneeze oceans
Propel my innards beyond the prison-drum of skin
To float less crystalline with Mesozoic ease
Express to the non-flesh
Beyond baneful smiles and barren sterile words

Better to ooze gaseous out of effort
Than to rot the corporate flesh

Blithe spirit of re-invented self arrest me
Mar the perfection of misery and reality
Scar the grafted skin
That life's insidious surgeon welds on us at birth
The flaccid birthright of carnality
That inflates our gratifying bellies at the dawn of youth

Camouflage the real marrow with filth
And of course you'll die from it
Give suck
Poison from the bruised breasts of motherhood

Sight-Sea

Solar glare
    Now splintered with lashes
        Lids orange with heat
            White crystalline noise

Lunar drag
    Chronos' shingles shifting
        Anonymous layers
            Usurp each other

Gripping the lonely instant
In the grim mosaic present

Chatter colliding
    Biped slumber
        Reclining the coastal couch
Sun blooms
    As if in recollection
        Trigger an electric giggle
            On permanent tanning frowns

Mirror of Mud

I offer myself
      For my own appraisal
This baggage
      Of conflicting impulses
And thickening impressions
      Can't save face

I am ashamed of my will
      To exist
In my reflection
      Of others

Self-imprisonment
The bars are bent
      Perfectly for escape
But I choose to hide
      In my own image
Shall I risk all I know
      To change?
Or confide
      In my own long shadows?

Shall I write my own plot?
      But what of my beginning?
What of my subject?
      What laceration of insight
Before I view myself
      More clearly?

Words
      From the heart
Or anonymously compiled
      For false impression
Blockage
      Filter the nutrients of thought
Debase it
      Dilute it
Then sprinkle it kindly on my fears

Screen Door

Worthless patterns in gauze
Obstruct immediacy of eye to object
Hexagonal diced reality
Part barricade – part frame

So too the worthless verse
Iambic snares – imprisoned tropes
Dancing hieroglyphic madness
To illume and then obscure

Disciple Dare

Jointly
Wash the silver, imposing hand
Through synopsis
And apocalyptic dream
Made more variant
As espionage
And its callous labour
Cumbersome
Strikes its mad appeal
Run forth
Amok
Finger gouging wind
Forcing the incandescence
Of tongue and god
Blunt
Eroded
With sleight of foot
Bookish in the light
Road
Eats impulse
God at the poet's ankle
Demure and laughing
At sad anglers on the kerb

Double Negative

I don't like spotted Medusas
Lifting obscene bailiff-like smiles
Through key-holes in London
With apparitions glaring
On Whitman's shopping lists
Bells chiming in rhymes
Eyebrows tilting clouds

I don't fear baboon barbers
Coiling tree-pole pranks
On limp-fingered kings
Whilst neutered popes guess
With schisms on their knees
Forging angry seams
To file their latent charges

21ˢᵗ Century David

A solitary stone
     slicing through serenity
Fragile watery surface
     madly broken and undone

Once sleeping river
     convulsing with intrusion
Vomiting its mild disturbance
     silver spray on wind

A pacified boy
     enthralled beneath splashes
Four more tainted giggles
     sadly swallowed in the deep

A solitary stone
     heart-bound within a sling
Tossed in for banal smiles
     beneath giant shadows of regret

Tears of the Drowning Man

Shrill pierce
       trumpet on wind
              collides with non-existence
Man fingers his way
       groping for ocean
              head thrashing with horizons
Two-tone blue meshes wet
       ducts filled with salted spite
              throat drowning with thirst
Brick-limbs sighing
       lungs pumped with gold
              slow not to the liquid lunatic

              Left limp to explode

Shadow of the Scythe

Destitute
Tawny ribbons in wind

Eyeless knotting on the sun
Brilliant and infinite suspension
Burning eternity through the belfry

Resilient
Bloody clusters on the shrub
Clutching with death-grip love

Limp fingers of splintered vegetation
Lifeless carrion under murderous eyes

Festering
Emotional discomposure
Life and vegetation churned

Equanimity
The barrel opens
Unleashing last vitalities

Life
Human chaff
Enter the sky

The Giggle - A Life

The giggle erupts
    boisterous on its leash

The chest vexes
    calamity of joy

Laughter
    weighed in gallons
        bellows the initial burst
            then snaps its neck

on the thread
        of its own invitation

Gorge of Senses

I strolled around that gorge of senses
Just to cleanse this myopic eye
 from shards of academia
 Dissolve preparatory cataracts
 as a salted snail

And how the eternal green of soft maternal forests
 Lined with splendour-tipped fantasies
 Unburden the lamp
 of its ocular weighted oracles

Mere simplicity
 Engendered within the close refines
 of starboard scrutiny
 Half-lit copses
 where peepers of inducted wisdom
Must
 See by touch – and Feel by history
 the soft – but comic – currents of the ether

 Paralyzing the aerial canopies
 with the clop of epidemic fog
This beauty swims in my experience
 like discarded roses in the culvert

 Just beyond that foreclosed thicket
Where kamikaze eyes
 Cast their visual fingerprints
 on that eraser of the human spirit
         Pain

 but how the dryad of greying elms
 Embalmed in sifting silence
 Provides me the half-cocked arrogance
 needed to beat back the panorama of paranoia
 that surrounds me with its tight army voice

 yet somehow
I am slightly pleased
 Captured in this purblind pastoral
 that howls on in angry-clown silence

Ruin

Shadows swept by a silent wind
Only to stain in a wall unbuilt
All I can do is sit in spacious hollow
To precipitate the expanse within

The acutest corner summons to brood
Shaded from the ragged light
In time's disease, a cradled whim
Inadvertently, blossoms crude

Decrepit fort laden bare
As a soul in sad decay
Why offer a seat for obstinacy
To refute this fateful disrepair?

The Forest Kiln

Just peruse the red-rail's ankle
Leaving cysts in the mud
And debauchery as wide-eyed as tree-stumps
Finding some anti-septic satisfaction

Here is autumn in whimsical flight
Clocked in rancid trails of heat
Foreclosing in mad, epic dissatisfaction
Its revolving curses, akin with wind

And now, holes in the dirt-clod
Avian tattoos swimming in the glare
Your ankle-print walled hillocks
Your cooing perversions
All gloating with the vagrant's smile

Miming pleasance in the steam
Mad-capped and caught
Imprints of winter's future kiss
And saliently, fruit withers

Protholic

Whirring of sound
    cluttered confession
        retorting dentures
           and magnesium prayers
These credo wails
    cant disturbances
        under godly winks
           in despotic priest's eyes
Give in
    give in
        then out

Remnants of old thoughts
    Blown through the bellows
Hydrogen breath
    on placid prophet guesses

Carriage Car

There's room in this carriage car
    for your splintered smile
Our landscapes clash through stolen reflections
Our outgoing tides tell of bruising losses
Your ship-wrecked eyes
    bleed on the jagged rocks
And this jarring locomotion,
Under bloodied sky of dreams
This hurtling chamber
Where destinies clash with evening

I know of a moonlit garden
    where cypress trees grow tall
A magic stream runs therein
    and quenches the thirst of us all

There's room in this carriage car
    for your receding words
Our tracks adjacent but destined never to meet
Enveloping motion
    that we might have been lovers
Aborted gazes
    now puddle on the sandy breach
The infernal onward
Our emerging black shadows
This careening tomb
And the newness of oblivion

I know of a moonlit garden
    where cypress trees grow tall
A magic stream runs therein
    and quenches the thirst of us all

In a Church of Flaunting Ghosts

Church
Where an anxious tenor lost his way
His eyes wandered
Off the script
So I rolled them down the aisle
And watched
A bulbous steward trip

Causing
The windows to tilt
Menacingly
So I righted them
And grinned
At the languid reflection
Left limping on my skin

Autopsy

Love threatens
    every form of torture
Love discloses
    every single fear

Manufactured in glances
    or wooing words
So much for one
    yet so little for another

That loss of moment
    that foreclosure of desire
A complex of energy
    in dismantled contact
Now neatly folded
    and damned in the giver
This somatic kiss
    and blank repose

Needling the Priest

What is this?
A glint upon the preacher?
The sacrificial clown
His eyes abuse the splendour
Of faces all around

Hold still!
The words of supposition
Grab histrionic throats
The fingered inquisition
Accrued in Godly gloats

Defy me
The scripted hallelujah?
Winking through the veils
Hold back the automatic mercy
Beg a penance for your tales

I'm nailed!
To Luther's sodden thesis
I'm scourged!
By Calvin's choosing hand
I'm blackened!
By Judas' thirty pieces
And softly kissed
By Jesuit demand

My choice
A bloody crucifixion?
Because now I can't face the lions
Who prey with Pharisee conviction
Smile with bloodlust on their shrines

So now
I excommunicate your sneers
And smash the rule box on your head
And Christ,
A man of queers, whores and sinners
Removes the telling needle,
Through which your soul cannot thread

Unconsigned

Soul
Oblique as scandalous words
Slices through object
Splinters of itself
Beyond disease
Through a state of obstinate oblivion
A demerit of our finest senses

Soul
My paltry shining offering
Crammed madly through prison bars
Bruised blue with admiration
The soft brutal movements
Of the siren

Face of the Deep

Bitten by the activity of shame
I washed my hands in the silver ashtray of time
And asked God
   "Whither thou goest?"
I lapsed for a while
   stumbling on bricks of silence
Then wheeled my fantasy towards me

Calm it comes
   calm and foreboding
Slow and certain
   acquiescent on the leash of time

Nod on
   in sleep
Nod on
   to star-widths of fancy

Birth to the new universe
In the slums of the old
Colour and shape your orgiastic importance
Under the skin-dome of a sleeping lid

"Dear God
   do I invent your deity?"
"Do I breathe life
   into an unseen grin?"

How do we carouse and dance with unbelief
Yet cringe under the looming shadows
Of future godly footfalls?

In the pantomime
   in the mental auditorium
"I gave you form
   you gave me void"
"I gave you flesh
   you gave me darkness"

Disappear

Eternal the moment
Shiver in synthesis
Eyes feel the heat of your renegade smile

I call
    You come
I wonder
    You shine
Then you disappear

Disappear

Dashing with colour
Writhing for emphasis
Edge of the night on the blanch of your skin

Oh pull us together
Power of ambivalence
Twist the dark shadows that yearn to be one

I ruse
    Your space
I linger
    To trace
Your memory

Memory

Spare me the perfume
Of timeless illusions
Clutching for midnight on the crow of dawn

Enduring the promise
Of shattered polarity
Love lies in drifts of the silent snow

Apparition?

Was it through the cotton balls of sleep
That I lay in the soft coils of your hair?
Was it your tiny yet all-encompassing hands
That tenderised my body to its core?
Did I really feel the blank rhythm
Of your full-moon gaze?
On the edge of your blood-pulsing lips
Enshrine myself in cloud-numbing softness?
You – a secret apparition?
You – an anonymous cooing siren?
I – entranced in your relieving touch?
Like silk on the bruises of my battered soul
Oh – what ripeness of spirit
Succulent under my tongue
And what warmth and fullness of content
That brings friction to my anxious senses
And how often did I find myself reclining
In the pearl-velvet reception of your flesh?
Your hands un-man me in delirious circles
And thirst my youth with the dew of desire
Your lazy eyes put my breath in recession
'Till I evaporate in your fire
You and I – exotic dancing shadows
On the fringe of delirious fear
Wild nerves – sequestered with shy beauty
Shiver in nocturnal joy

Shafted

Trapped in a mine
      the cavernous deep
My soul is eclipsed
      by the darkness of silence
Shards of my past
      tear at my face
I'm bludgeoned
      by the act of continuous repentance
Is there a tunnel
      that leads to a light?
Is there a purpose
      as hard as this goal?

Inlet Drift

Mesmerising dream
    Enchanting vision
        Mirror of fantasy
            Magnet to whims

Is it with you I stand
    Enmeshed like an eternal painting?
Two loves of no time
    Two lovers of unreality

I travel your pulsating current
    And feel the perplexity of the ocean
Straining to heave its bulk
    At the winking Luna's beckoning

Is it with you I lay?
    Floating in your shapely shadow
Feeling the magnanimous roar
    A turbulent sea in my limbs

My lungs fail me
    I succumb to a delicious drowning
In the secret lagoon
    Of my forbidden nymph

What ripple in my thoughts
    What seduction to freedom
        What dream surreal
            What vision corporeal

Watery den of make-belief?
    Or elopement with discovery?
What oceanic mystery have I befallen?
    inavigable logic and reason?

You internal myth
    Goddess of my sleeping eyes
Enchantress of the stars
    If only I could wake to dream again

The Deep

She loves me blindly
Without any purpose
Her lips are blunt
As cold as stone

Eyes like a pond
Placid and weightless
She plunges me in
No ripples surround
She plunges me in

Primordial

YOU
The traveller of distance
FEEL
Your breath fill out the night
YOU
Saunter like the evening sun
DANCE
On the waves of your plight

GROW
Mighty with his purpose
TRANSFORM
Amongst the colours
There is no loss that you can't face
My father
Son
and brothers

In this immeasurable darkness,
BE
That power of encounter
And whisper to the silent earth
YOUR NAME
WHISPER
To the silent earth
YOUR NAME

Your blood like mighty oceans
RUN
To the corners of the world
Your voice cajoles the thunder,
CRASH
With the wondering words
I AM
With the wondering words
I AM

Autumnal

That time of year
    In you behold
Your russet eyes
    Are cold
        My love
My voice is but
    A falling leaf
That circles to
    Your feet
        My love
And laying there
    A token bare
    For you
        My love
In serving you
    Reduce me to
        My love

We know the rains will come
    Thunder crash
    Like a bomb

Winds will blow so carelessly
    But strong the roots
    Of our tree

The sunset fades
  Your face again
Your silhouette
  Clings to
    My love
The last leaf
  On the twisted tree
On bended knee
  For you
    My love
And idolise
  My only prize
  That's you
    My love
In serving you
  Reduce me to
    Your love

Inhumanation

Notice the way the sky turns black
The weight of the snow, the branches crack
The frozen trail of a mother's tear
The angry hands on the ice-cold bier

Notice the guilt in the siblings near
The pity and stench of selfish fear
The oblong shadow gliding past
The silhouette of a cancelled past

Notice the way they rub their hands
The nervous way they cling to the land
The reticence of a distant bell
The cloying bark of this death knell

Notice the ones that turn away
With the falling ash and the falling clay
The sated lust and the secrets kept
Locked away in the icy crypt

Three colours mark the grave
Tricolour on the stony pave
Flying like an ancient flag
Locked upon this hardening crag

See the quiver of betrayal
See the stance of denial
There upon the hallowed ground
Here beyond the quick and the found

Ice Flower

Yuki-onna

White princess, do you cry
When lonely tears, snow now falling?
Primal sorrow, what become?
Frozen tears, a mourner's calling
Tragedy in banks of white
No relent, a dark foreboding
Pain of love, crystalline
Weeps for me, avalanche imploding
Goddess gentle, now ferocious
All is buried by the evening
Yet still she weeps, unrequited
Her deity of endless grieving

Abandoned there where all is shining
The frozen lake for lost love
Find someone else in the thawing
They'll elope to the sun
When many winters merge together
I find myself on the shore
A silhouette marks the distance
But yesterday is nevermore
Yet still she stands ever shining
Time unravished in a cold sun
A lover spurned, my guilt's companion
An icy beach on which to run

Kori-no-hana

Babbla

I hear the wordless words
Articulated sweetness
Brilliant light of fancy
Where every sound deserves a kiss

The treetops tinged with sunlight
Where Elven councils gather
Where streams gather force
And Vikings seek their plunder

Energy in random
Thoughts we cannot gather
Strange remote abandon
From a distance we can savour

I hear the songless song
Wisdom in its fullness
Boundaries unravel
Delicious unsureness

In miniature glory
Secret dreams deliver
Worries wonder mute
And mortality a sliver

Golden glow surrounding
Halo strange and splendid
Bouncing bliss unfurling
Innocence untended

Giants met with venom
Monsters racked with anguish
Melodies unguarded
And mirth, a silent language

I hear the wordless words
Articulated sweetness
Brilliant light of fancy
Where every sound deserves a kiss

Sylvan Forest

Along tide a dream
The autumn downy tresses
Sing with silver haloed sunlight
Their blithe songs do stream
Though fjords of boyish charm
As sure as sample blood
Courses through a father's veins

He Grew Bogus

Cowboy skull 'n' bones
Intelligence a bust
A 'decider' in his dreams
A puppet for manipulation
Lazy thief of power
An earpiece for his God
A leader of an arrogant nation

Cronies stuff the courts
Toadies hack the news
Control defines the patriot
War profit for the King

Bully of the nations
Torture for the Righteous
Eavesdrop on the innocent
Drowning of the downtrodden

Fear as a weapon wielded
Lobby for a slice of pie
Oil for the blood of peasants
Tycoon taxcuts given here

Stall while the world is warming
Trash family privacy
Deny that the nation's ailing
Kick a poor man to the ground
Thumb your nose at older culture
Steal from your children's trust

Unilateral executive
National guard pretender
Ground zero posturing
Drunken crusader

Bailout prince of racketeers
Disparager of freedom
Swiftboat morals for a preacher
Drunken crusader

The Pretender

I parked the car and walked the back streets
Fighting the rigours of my conscience
Moon shadows on terraced gardens
Danced upon my agitation
Threshing out the seeds of memory
Coming to the same conclusions
About you

Kaleidoscopic is my world view
I don't know what to make of it
Colours clash in the prism
The single cry of a screech owl
Slices through preoccupation
Struggling for revisions here
About you

I walk until I reach the morning
Sparkling on an old horizon
Orange orb on the precipice
Inviting new renditions
Searching for new history
Looking for new memories
About you

I cut a straight line to the future
Past the stares of old acquaintance
Through the market of redemption
Trinkets traded above their value
I'm walking by without a second thought
Abandoning the mystery
That is you

MEmorial

Always
In the temple of your smile
I see windows
   teem with golden boughs
I swim rivers
   of the greatest ease
      Always
Just within reach
I feel rainbows
   softly under my tongue
The ocean caresses my face
      Always
In remembrance of you

Mystical Eyes

Mystical Eyes, poised and socketed
With velour movements
And glassy introspection
Deep ochres cum forgotten greens
Globular dazzle in ephemeral streams
Plush penumbra and fragmenting pain
Over-visual synapse, ocular terrain
Festooned orbs, munificent gaze
The allure of chance
The magnet of caress
The atonement of retinal scans
The wash of the velour

Dream me from the pinions of comfort
Mesmer and dalliance
Centrifugal moons
Spilled complicity
Eyelet smiles
Dream on a subordinate tear

Staggering Space

There's a cipher
Goes through water
Singular dweller
Crystalline ice
Steam sensations
Impact of voices
Serpents of vapour
Ambits from the sun
Reversed lunar forge
Hissing snails
Clairvoyant love
Voided repose
Didactic prism

Aspects of a name
Compound is the word
Insular sound
Vocal modification
Endlessness
Transpiration
Migratory
Interior monsoon
Ballet in the balance
Doctrinal ruse
Voice is essence

The optical nerve
The inverted current
The trampoline sorrows
The oracle of cataclysm
The nadir of wind

Mirage vortex
Stolen eruption
Variable x-rays
Pre-ordained reversal
Voided furnace
Spectral goddess
Desert nebulae
Ruing ghosts
Sacrificial volcano
Staggering space
Staggering space

Langue Secrète

Miorstabur, i strat masurk
Iviermart sol i makhine
Sturamakar siel matorpic
Iravin plaki mekarboliche
vuatu bairn sivliar sikama
tensuk alakyipa esaravoo
defardmir salak ivwarm tek
sinli vukat i slek urn sivlur

Orchan

Rivalry of sea cows
Slipstream turbulence
Monolith notions
Tankard breath
Retention of bellows
Fraught porcelain
Submerged ballooners
Nether-touch caresses
Blimpian nuzzles
Oceanic bassoons

Fireworks at Makr al-Deeb

The sun settles on the Rubiyah flats
Ochre hues flitting on the sifting granular mounds
Where the scant paths of smugglers and refugees
Spider like slightly traceable veins
Across the crenellated Mesopotamian basin
Now divided between Syria and Iraq

Against the backdrop of a bruising sky
A bride, vestal white and newly hennaed
Love-giddy from the Lailit fest
The sinews of youth angular against the gown
Gives herself to the last eddies of an old Chaldean dance
And a groom, bluebottle shark-skinned
Leans against the shoulder of the old toothless Pashtun organist
In a moment of quiet repose

It is on the precipice of future past
Between these two dusky colonial trinkets of Britain and France
Along this old Persian fissure between Sunni and Shia
That the polytonal dance of the Dabka
Gives way to a celebratory Kalashnikov crackle
Mere pinpricks in the canopied ether
As an undivided silhouette descends to a nuptial tent
Where Ibrahim and Sarai once tangled in perfumed consecration

The families sleep on blankets festooned with traded amulets
And the scraps of a dishevelled wedding cake
The Qaim lapses into long-short shadows
As the moon nictitates through laddered Arab clouds

Silent vacuum blast and face melting heat flash
Corpuscular over-pressure and axial skeleton hammers
A demented pianoforte on the concert grande of ambush
Initial explosion birthing vortex implosion

As the solar hurricane air drag-suck catapults neatly pruned human logs
Into a Neo-Nebuchadnezzan furnace

Atmospheric overlap peels fingers like plantains
To smouldering bone and useless fractured pivots
Searing eyelid membranes blinding gelatinous skull orbs
Blood boils in balloon busted lungs
The detonations spiral in radial anger
Dragging indiscriminate husks of children along their trajectory
To a buckled landing of dust and gore

Chinooks gather in the sky like evening gnats
Then send hydrodynamic arrows into the fray
Which like angry pistons push and compress
Against innocent bulwarks of flesh
Such neat compressions against escapist fervour
As spherically expanding pressure shocks
Find a human hair wick to an awesome array
A supersonic fireball, an all-consuming torch

Human candles spend their centrifugal force
Aerial repeaters perform, pyrotechnic pirouettes
Firecrackers, ground spinners, Boom-flowers and fountains
Poppers and smoke bombs, snakes and sparklers

Fireworks. Fire works!

Blood-gargled screams of survivors pierce polyrhythmic blasts
And hot gaseous residues gnaw at last mumbled prayers
They run and stumble, dragging carcasses like pathetic ants
Across sacked families alabastered in death
They seek the circumference of miasma
But no margins here, only moving epicenters
Only the slow combustion of heart and hope
As ground troops volley into those that dare to crawl or weep

Somewhere amid these stumbling Andronici
Among the zombied children of ruptured memory

71

Between the useless rope and tendril of spilt entrails
A dying voice death rattles your name – America

"Shock and Awe"
Rapid dominance, overwhelming power
Visual array of force
Dumbshow, peepshow
A conqueror's slick nomenclature
Sun Tzu's shiny warring epigram
Plagiarized from the sloganeering textbook of Goebbels
Repackaged for your mass media lobotomization
"Shock and Awe"
The wit of the self-congratulates
The poetry of the sneering playground bully
Buzzwords, soundbites, catchphrases, doctrines in minutiae
As proliferate as raining bombs on Sunni bridesmaids

Shock and Awe – give us more
Our unrequited bride of violence

The matriarch with meatless pearloid eyes
Locked in her catatonic death stare
Carrier of myths and dreams
Now the broken vessel of truncated history
A recently proud father
Neck unhinged by a hot iron shingle
The unmitigated dowry of a neatly decapitated soul
An anonymous youth
Unzipped from chin to groin by shrapnel razor
Ribcage like the moon-blanched frayed rigging
Of a long abandoned ghost-ship
Charred cherubim
Lips still welded to a mastectomised nipple
Blood and milk mottle on the dark desert floor
Your stars and stripes – America

America – with your acrid desert shrub leader
Your haemorrhaged notions of vengeance

Your self-epistulatory histrionica
America – with your posturing barons
Your media mogul harems
Your blood wedding feast erotica
America – with your Armageddon lust
Your water-boarding heart
And gluttonous teenage soul
With your legions of AmeriChrists
Blue-eyed, nether-cheeked militants
Come to bring the rusty Norman sword
to yet another vacuous crusade
Once the mighty Saladin – now the humble village parade

Shock and Awe
Shop and score
Shock and Awe
Cock and whore
Shock and Awe
Lop and gore
Shock and Awe
Fuck and lure
Shock and Awe
Give us more

No neatly hidden coffins to discard the refuse
Just a Syrian flatbed lorry stacked with butchered remains
Thinly crêped in blood-soiled sheets
And limbs still arched in latent embrace
27 dirt-clod graves, 40 hurriedly scribbled names
Amputee orphans in the humid nursery
Of simmering rage and hate

The Scream

Woodblock miasma in Munchian dislocation
Sine wave clouds over ovaline lake

Two double masted boats meet end to end
Two shadowy strollers down the three-railed bridge

Curative androgyne foregrounded and frozen
Elliptic mouth covets, a titular fury

Yet both hands bar the ears' authorial reception
Downward grains – uniplumes of the sunken

Printlines mute with wooden retraction
Scalpel blunt from the hardness of intention

Desire

Always
        on like the obdurate sun
Always
        remiss with orphanic yearning
Always
        tangled as the fingers of a sagebrush
Always
        lost like a flag in the fog
                        Always

Tribal Voids

The residue of candour
    In waxen trails across the skin
The chakras on opined virtue
    Damned on the tongue
Resplendent to the eye
    Left pining for the abyss
All saturnine, titular glory creeps
    Aging by its own intent
And the last ghostly walks
    Of its shackled condemnation

Depointed

There is a fuselage across the ceiling
Metallic plunder, yesterday's trinket

There's foliage in my ether
Phosphorescent gloating, tomorrow's thicket

Xenomarket

Rust drum, spherical dance
Over-tailed and über-horned
Limbs spigot and peacock fancy
Eternal embrace in vermillion dream

These sightless ephemera
Sidecar to its careening culturation
This circumference of miasma
On the rim of pretence

Trappist

Benedictine drifts
The assemblage of pliancy
Dropsied curtsey
The fallout of words

Ubar

I came through effervescence
And boiling stupor
To find you recalcitrant
Over-yielding to foregone guilt

I moved through centrifugal forcefields
And beguiling redux
To find you shaken
Over penetrative to bygone fear

Albion Twine

There was once a time where the Thames and the Seine were one and I kissed you many times on its banks. Through the foliage of the boxgrove, I came to know how you spangled in the late afternoon sun, where the equines ran and laid smooth our bed.

And as the last glaciers melted, we smelled the breathing pines mixed with birch and alder on the sunset breezes. We watched the Auroch rut in the ferns between kisses and courted the moon in each other's eyes. Twixt the henges, where we often frolicked, you once bound me and swore your love eternal, whispered its softness over the old chamber tombs that guard the old secrets.

The land was ours when Pytheas skirted the coast and the raiders pummelled the hill-forts in an effort to rent us twain. But nothing could us sever, that which is forever fused; not the Celt incursion, the Latin scourge, nor the savages from the Jutlands. We were entwined upon the first sun and so shall be upon the last sinking moon. We were circled in chalk, morrissed at the maypole, and purified under the Queene of heaven's smile.

You once leaned me against the ancient oak of wonder and kissed my eyes, promising me that the Norns would be kind to us. I ran with the deersmen to claim that promise, followed the horn to the wishing tree, which has left my heart in shadow ever since. And now that we are in a new time and have found each other again, I must place the bawm and the garland given to me that day, place it on the one that knew my soul in its forging. I must abide the three heartbeats in the quest to claim what I have desired to be eternal, brace the elementals to the bower of binding.

For we were made and joined on this land, from the wolds, to the plains, to the downs, to the dales, on the moors, and deep in the gorges. We are old spirits of the Brython, locked forever in Lloegrian love, a love that has borne and will bear each other through the labyrinthine.

Sudden Poetry Corner

Pray… what is sudden
In the birthing vortex that is Poesy?
Where evolutions posture their eternity
And yet mollify the slatterns of the present
With nothing but a palsied kiss

And what corner of fractured light
Amidst the dancing motes of words
Where airless frolic stupefies the moment
And fails to capture the bleeding remonstrations
Of the muses' midwife, hanging o'er
The cold and ruddiless still-born

How angular the corner
With its shielding walls and insular margins
Trapping the half-light
And sifting through the mottled memories
Of the newly damned and nether-virtuous
Clinging to the nipple of gesture

Where is the fractious instant?
At what moment can we take truck with the crime?
Which hand of chronos falters for the stop-gap seer
Crooked like a scythe over the poverty of his language
With what breath can we anchor the purpose
Affix the meaning, gratuitously plucked
From the folds of a soul's corner?

Words… mere prosthetics of sonic announcement
The air that pulls the rope and bone
Caught in rattles and clutches
Somewhere above the infanticide heart
That is poetry

Spume to Illume

Last radial arcs meduse the twilight sheen
Mute inamorta shadows summon to the loom
Milk marbled opacity that drifts on the tides
Sweep the millioned shingles as fingers ply satin

She lays him down in the fluxotine caress
The nape of the sea where the eddying sluices run
And hands gather in their formless whirlpool touches
To disrobe the last circumscriptions that dare to rag the soul

And now astride his driftwood frame, the cilium chain descends
All carmine grace like wounds upon the moon
A rosette to pool around the floodless beating hub
That spates the grill with all the rigours of an ocean

Enamelline light is the sheathing of desire
The tumbling titian tress frames the lover's shy embrace
Undulating billows break across the entwining respires
That catch like dusk on the rim of the sky

Deep in her eyes the tawny sorrels run
Ambit whorls that holds the beauty in
The mouth's magenta promise, inlet flush with calm
Soft crepuscular touch, an orb upon the brine

The lamps cancel out with the closing of their eyes
Last draperies of night enshroud the vulnerable forms
Tenement undertows lap the lovers out
Laced penumbra lattice on the twitches of the sea

Prayer to the Veiled One

Oh how can I contain you in such a vessel chamber
When you are the light that finds charcoal in my bones?
What garden of bliss befalls this dumb initiate
That the tatters of pride should bend to sip at the inchoate moon?

All my nights are but a rude gown of proffered splendour
Where shadows traded are merely the scions of the fanciful
And now, like a tendril wave you come to placate my dying youth
As a reticent beam through my spectral age with all the rapier's lust

I am made low by the fallows of my wanton state
Where an age of granite dissolves to nether-motes on your breath
Only to yield to the rigours of that surely dance unto death
All clamouring under the hallowed folding of your eyes

Oh forgive this vain ventriloquy in the stretch for your favour
Overlook my vestal verse in the vain tracery of reverence
I seek the language of Azazel
I pluck the fork from Lavinia's mouth
I filch Bruno's last burning cry
And find sustenance in the Babelian collapse

It is just my frenzied look for corpus
In the embers of my sacrifice to you
As the fractal yearnings of my song
Find glossary in your beauty

Tonight, the garden finds you in lumin colour
And I hold fast in your lunar veins
As Arachnae to her silken chains
All suspended in drunken animae

And still the shimmer of your munificent glass
Finds refraction in my sunken eyes
Where death is peepshow to the future
But dare not bare his darkened hand

Infinity erupts when I find your gaze
And Aleph yields the death-grip prize
The integer rounds the sharpening stone
Before the numeral dagger finds an edge

I am given to the phantoms of duenna
In the soft bartering for my desire
For you are the my sole priestess
On this tantric yet brazen star

Oh polarity of my satellite heart
Draw my binary states in union
Invade my deeper storm
With the axioms of your benevolence

Let me be worthy in this cleft of chance
Bound by nothing but a silver thread of hope
Allow me to wade the shimmering pool
That calms the billion ethers of my heart

Fabula

Rooted, the stolid bulb nestles in the causeless
As obsidian shadows dance across the damask
Where all is rain in the furthest pinions of the sky
As a circular stone collects silver ion whispers

She is crepuscular, waif-shrouds among forest fingers
A dancer's gate that dare not crack the venal clay
Sends alabaster petals along the last simoom
That breathes incarnadine the volleys of love

Woven in lights to the histones in my bones
Where blizzards of desire spend their downy fury
The labyrinthine foci of enveloping chambers
Blasts a single flower upon the green

We evil

They go through prayer like termites
   at the old plank of a tumble down church
      Plotting their immaculate conceptions
         amid the ruins of wish fulfillment
         Worms in dead sojourn
            eating through their own vain corruptions
      The lust feast of the nether-damned
at the nailed feet of last hope

Mooted Mute

My words
    Are
The poverty
    Of
    My
True intentions

Intentions true
    Mine
Of poverty
    Are
My words

In the Valley of the Meuse

Circumlocution of waifs
Effluvium in shadows
All spectral this nether-calm
A billet of thickets
Cradle old soldier dreams

Croak of expiration
Rattle in the final clutches
The sequined stars care naught for the lampless eye
Nor the shapely rigors of the dead
Damning up the river

What requiem for dithering attrition
Reciprocity in the dying gaze
Verdun in dark velvets
Nocturnal cloak for death-naked shame
Quiet kiss of sleepless repose

Boethus

What moment caught your fancy?
Was it the first startle to the grip?
Was it the elephantine eye under pressure?
Was it the hopeless flatter against closure?

What brought the chisel to the stone?
Was it the first collapse of innocence?
Was it the naked power of youth?
Was it the stance of the cheap conqueror?

Papaver Rhoeas

What shallow tomes for the dead?
The scarce slipped sentence
On recalcitrant tongues
The last winking glory
On the despot's weather-veined eye
The evicted word
Scarpered logoi on gone breath
The last exasp
The bloated gasp against absolute deflation

They wear poppies
Lapelled like enunciatory names
The garb of the plumeless
Against the corruption of memory
The roseate insignia of the fallen
Resplendent against the grey morn
The bell-ringer's fervour
Against the mute clank
of clapperless bells

Song of the Cephalon

Mummers and mumblers
All-convening remonstrance
Against the chosen void
All swaddling in the grave clothes
Of a spent urge
All petrified against
The glyphs of last collapse

Beaded wraiths
In lightless sepulchre
Cavorting ghosts
In breathless supplication
Dam against the damned

Offsprung

She bears me: misconception
Wingless plather, airless bird
Frugal beginnings: aborted lifts
All flap against shiftless weight

She rears me: misappropriation
Soundless phonetica, muted siren
Bankrupt intentions: lopped tongues
All stub against soundless objection

She ends me: miscarriage ration
Ruptured pump, seeping refrain
Cancelled solution; dismembered hope
All bulk against lifeless carnage

Escondig

You can still hear my canso against the wind
Modal exhalations of the trobar clus
Posited to the medius sea

Did it sheathe the holy roman sword
Raise the Marions and Cathars to elect
In vacant shadows of the Jongleur?

I would be your chansonnier still
Breathe insipid on the shore
Monophony from all your shells

Armageddon Lust

In the vortex where assassinations hatch
The slow birthing of upturned snarls
Consanguine pitch mottles at the points
The woodworm at the damn's last cross-hatch

In the vestry where murder becomes the intake
The pithy stigma that gums up the trachea
Larva hate seething at the tunnel joists
The spindle against the fathoms of hell

Death-grip Love

There is something in the clutch that is broken
An element of the clasp that is damned
Hand-chafery in the greeting
Peeling pads and splintered fingers
The drape before final collapse
The last augurs of the breathing
Sinews of bone against tautness
Angles of broken stone against frost

The Final Dowry

You, the gift-child of impotence
The trinket of drowning men
The oath sworn to buffoonery
The fetid stage of plague

Unfurl your last horror
Play the trump card of the damned
Roll the rotting rune on the warped table
Show us how beautiful you are

Marlais

For war-like tremens
They gave him morphine
Blew up his brain
And shut down his bronchioles
Did he submit to dominion
Pneumonic and blue?
Did he rise from the sea
Our lion of Wales?

Somnium Mihi Verus

You glide in like the aubade star
Damask of snow against vibrissa red
All porcelain grace and filament

You sense the wisps of my revenant soul
Transported fibres of corporeal haze
Reaching through the last adumbrations of night

You peer through the shifts of flightless air
A conjurer of shadows, an architect of shimmers
Against the voids of last absolutes

You shape my likeness from the marl of hope
An amorous eidolon mechanised through insistence
Respiring my ghost to attendance

You savour me through the shroud of our isolate star
Dream real the denouement of phantasm
And clasp me whole to your recondite heart

The Aeolian Catch

Shy whispers
　　Want to sing
　　　　Mustering the courage
Talam
　　First tear falls to earth
　　　　second to lips
Something
　　About that old wind-driven trunk
　　　　Bleaching in the sun
　　　　　　Hewn roots still the keeper of mysteries
Albho
　　wooden ear to time's chaconne
　　　　Caught secrets of the meadow
Windsong
　　Breathing counterpoint
　　　　Cajoled into mirrored states
Sloped hills
　　Calciphile fauna
　　　　Where buried fingers
　　　　　　Pluck the limestones
Round
　　leading tones leading
　　　　Old Beech doddering with age
　　　　　　Drystone serpents
　　　　　　　　Copper and gold strands intermingled
Some hollows
　　Made to be filled
　　　　Spaces that cradle the willing
　　　　　　Enticements that transcend
　　　　　　　　The dim actuals of presence
Windsong
　　Dare you sing?
　　　　sing to me?
　　　　　　Coloured tones on pushed breaths
Marsh Tit
　　leads the way
　　　　Jocular jackdaw
　　　　　　Chances a rasp on the breeze

Play for you
    Chords are a soft trident
        Pawing at the wolds
Ornamentation
    The subtle spaces
        Between the hedgerows
            Only for you
While you sleep
    Crescent panorama
        Form the gentle rises
We breathe
    The town-names
        In a way that conquers the ether
Nectar
    Honey in the scrub
        Cupped orchids nod their approval
B minor
    Even the stolid trunk
        Hums through its time-layered demise
How we live
    The cloven
        The rapt
            Sharers of the eternal round
                The mysterious sanctity of regeneration
Beechwood vibrance
    Upon scant-treed hills
        Carriers of the twining thread
            Daring to breathe
                Against the final cresting of sacred waters
Don't leave
    There's twin magic here
        The miniature fire of the stray poppy
            The dryad purpose against the skylight
Windsong
    This how I live my life
        You
            Me
                And the eternal birthing of our song

ωμέγα

My Desire seeks omega
A requiter's terminus
Some corporeal consummation
At longing's heel

Oh for the beflowering of wish
The suspire for fire
That yen of ardour
In vigorous colour blasts

I am all concave
Cavernous clefts
Sepulchral soundings
In the space that awaits you

My demarcate heart
Lurches circumscript
Towards the last hollows
Of void that calls your name

To the Luna Sensitives

I am no feckless jewel just hung on fancy's thread
I too am a tandem light, a mirroring orb
I reflect keenly and keep timely concealments
I shine in partial but hide purpose in my shadows

I am no fire of pale desire nor simply pearl the air
I too am a maker of currents, a stirrer of oceans
I pull you closer and magnetise what is willing
I wax your wanton heart and wane your brittle fears

You are natural satellites
You are orbitally locked
You are synchronous hearts
You are the peeling of shadow
You are the revealing of light
You must love through the eclipses

You seek me without when I am within

Luminosity

Where all is burnish at crepuscular light
Bled from the zenith star on the skein of night
Marble from the lip of shadow shines
Like moonspun tears down phosphor lines

Where all is lambent through her lustrous eyes
Resplendent orbs upon polished skies
Lucent moons silken to the cheek
That eyelash flutter all lovers seek

Where all is radiance in the penultimate touch
On the spindled moment before the clutch
She draws me to the candle flame
The refulgent spark from whence I came

The Marketable Seer

I am a pixilated dream
I am the midriff of the sun
I am the ocean's foment
I am a Euclydian moment

I have the sense of the damned
I have hieroglyphic toxicity
I have reputable sighs
I have dorian cries

Pastorelle

Cornflowers
    Marigolds
Scant poppy or two
    Dithering copse
Sun-gazing
    Fingerlet branches
Swanning breezes
    Forest stealth
No sound
    stoops to touch
Dew-moistened lips
    Solar-warmed neck
Shudder knows origin
    Lean into hungry lips
Make soft ellipses
    Chin and collarbone
Hands laced
    Conforming shapes
Searching mouths
    lean against ancient bark
Smooth with old lovers
    Hands on hips
Voice whimpers
    Fingers connect
Tracing lines
    Ribs and spine
Simultaneous slide
    Down old wizened trunk
Knees meet yellow rattle.
    Lips find home
Gently rocking
    Cowslips
Campion
    Balance yielding

Twining lips
    Plush mattress
Clover sown grass
    Mouth follows descent
Hair flows over
    Vermillion waterfall
Fingers loosen
    Everything yearns sunward
Kissing secret constellation
    Across heart
Down navel
    Hands lost
Sun-spangled tresses
    Return slowly
Breathing
    Yarrow tinged essence
Enveloped fullness
    Stammering name
Shying sun

A/V

Atomic plather
   Ubiquitous synthesis
      Eyes rapt with the schisms of focus
       Deplorable things
        Beatific remiss

Moon Couplets

As the pale rosette around the moon
Which rings at zenith its pearly rune
I shall bind to thee as petals cup their dew
And braid the reaching strands with light anew
As fronds to the soil. The willow's kiss
Finds for its thirst an eternal silver bliss
We shall cast our twin shales to the roots
And make our garland bed of Albion's shoots
There among the shunt of culvert streams
Conjoining prongs dowse the ancient dreams
The earthen grail bears the lover's lap
Nectar suckled fresh from nature's tap
A forth upon the river thou will be
Sweet beck that flows to my darkest sea

Wood Nymph

Oh she's light woollen... and how fingers might stray in the copse where the gnarled trees splay over her. Splendiferous in the primaries she is... as in black, white, or the absence of colour upon her naked hues. Bark to bark... full luna inversions... done in circular folds... inward slippage... eternelle.

Oh how plush in the lime-flecked dryads... you who put splendour in soft moving rhymes... who put iridescence at eye's end... morning spangle with eternally young suns. How she fits in moments... brilliant suspension... dual propped tree, woman... bipedular glory upon titular desires.

Oh the cross-hatching framery... the intent of shadows on nameless subjects... the bark that lines the fingers... knots of hand on wood... the elbows at branch comfort... convexed in twinings and perpendicular embraces.

Oh the figure among appendant figurines... the fullness that draws taut the gaze... the momentary emancipations of distant lovers... extensions of vine ethers and faerie furies... the drawn sap upon the hungry lips... the epoch of fancy where temptation forms its first cluster.

Oh the final commune... at the woods' heart... at the woodsman's dreams... where the bullrush lays down to the new river... the dark cotes where the hidcotes run... the final arrest of the iris... and the orphean orchid finds purchase in fingerlet shades... there is she, light woollen... fluted with upward impress... gongs in the clover sing out to the hills and call her name.

Graven

Upon the undulating chalk
Which seam the ocean churn
The touch of old limestone
Seems cold to the paramours

There in the lintern shadows
Cupped in causewayed hopes
Concentric rings tighten
Round the rosy dawnlet haze

The filling of earthen chambers
with rubicund filament
A pulse in blushened barrows
to cleanse nocturnal tombs

What passage from the iron
A slaughter-stone reversal
The Beaker heart rewarmed
Soft phosphor kiss on henge

When sarsen shades are blackest
And sinister pitch is all
The trueloves in the recess
Await the wands of morn

Phantasy

I want to share the same impress
    The hollows subsume the shape
I want to braid the filament rope
    The twin medullas bind
I want to feel the labial clasp
    The joined respire of love
I need your ether silken drum
    The pulsing of my dreams

Mary's Lake

Cragged curtains drawn
Backs to the wind
Rippled gestures collect
In spirals of dancing shadows
Deep lake eyes
Spy the murmurs of morning
Through the ochre sunsheen
Where the deep snows ran
Phosphorescent circumlocution
Lap the mottled shoreline
Where the Arapahoe sang

Hydropaddle

Sploos, Merc, Dilk
Spauline drifts
Radial light arcs
Milk-mead runs
Toes are the conductor
Meld to the melt
Equaline redux
Scarp along the scurries
Tlem, Lupp, Tlee
slunk blue quadroons
Dune plathered vortex
Spangle-made riddles
Iridescent aquadreams

Propelle

Storkine girl
    Spindle trawler
        Legs fluted white
    Stilted quiet repose
        Single stance
            Locked fledgling poles

Epon)a

Milk)en(shroud)ed(
Hoof)en(spool)ed(
Arc)ade(whinny)ing(
Twine)d(run)ner(
Chalk)ed(dream)t(
Garland)ed(tr)ea(od
Moon)y(man)ed(
Mare)d(night)ly(

uilleann

Inflate me
Cradled bag
Bellows sucked
Stuck-waisted
Under your right arm

Blow me
Ballooned lung
Dry-breathed
Reeds blasted
Under your hung tongue

Sing me
Sweetened tone
Range-chanted
Drone regulated
Closed at your wrists

Grace me
Staccato rasp
Tone-holed
Air strangled
Flaccid on your thigh

Pitiless

Desedged
Unbirded
Oversquirreled
Unharvested
Rosefaded
Quickwithered
Lightfooted
Wildeyed
Lovestared
Moansweetened
Songbended
Faesung
Strangespoken
Trueloved
Eyeclosed
Quadrakissed
Dreamsodden
Hillfrosted
Pitycried
Thrallgotten
Wakefound
Chillhilled
Lakewithered
Unsung

Pep Tide

Dorsalin love
    The Acropoline surge
        Stone recalcitration
            Rivers unbended
        Half light of umbrage
    In seething straights
Past strychnine choirs
    Bevelled rejoinders
        Aft mortification
            Fuselage fears

Oneiroi Open House

Please come
Roam around at will
Visit the granary
Where the family loom is kept
Visit the colandrine loft
Where the rain seeps in
Visit the mind field
Where the implosions unfurl

Please come
Infiltrate my dreams
Visit the winery
Where the baubs are let
Visit the dredge pond
Where the currents are damned
Visit the brain paddock
Where the centaurs run blind

Tetrapodular Assent

Salamander
>	Stuck-toed belief
>	Four and five trod
>	Water dream propulsion

Salamander
>	Regenerative faith
>	Skin and tail shod
>	Colour scheme redemption

Ascent

Ah
To be lifted
Hoisted
Aloft
To the point of soar

I love
The feel
Of lifting hands
The coil
Of purposeful fingers

I love
That moment
Where the breath
Catches
Where the filament
Flares in the eyes

That clasp
That locking
Before uplift intention
The point of knowing
Of recognition
Of surrender

The anchoring
Of limbs
Before the final
Thrust ascension
The stance
In the shadow
Of the act

Bearing
Beyond the boost
Building to buoy
The soft mount
Heavenward
In the heft of love

Folly

I am fill
Where quarries fail to plunder
I am full
Where clouds are rent asunder
I am fell
Where glades succumb to plunder
I am fall
Where winds are left to blunder

Genea

You know me by my towpaths
My echoes strewn with brine
The way I carry narrowboats
And water gypsy time

You fashion me with locks
And send me shunting north
A weaver in the sluices
With a shadow standing forth

About the Author

Daniel Staniforth is an English writer, composer, and teacher now residing in Lafayette, Colorado. Recently serving for three years at the Jack Kerouac School of Disembodied Poetics' Summer Writing Programme, Daniel now works at Naropa University and is a part-time English faculty member at the Metropolitan State College of Denver. Daniel earned a Master's degree in Literature from Miami University (of Ohio) and writes poetry, fiction and literary analysis. His theoretical work, *Ontological Mirrors and the Rite of the Godgame: Theological Components in Twentieth Century Fiction* is forthcoming from Skylight Press in 2011. As a multi-instrumentalist and composer, he writes, records, and produces alternative, classical, and experimental music (including "sonic poet-scapes"). His recordings include works by Luna Trick, Alchymical Muse, Rebsie Fairholm, Dream nth, as well as orchestral pieces under his own name (released by Flowforth Productions/Sonic Spongecake Records). His music with Rebsie Fairholm has featured in theatre productions at the Cheltenham Playhouse Theatre and the National Media Centre in Nathupur, India, as well as two feature films directed by John Hartman. Their music videos for various songs, orchestral pieces and poems are available on YouTube. Daniel has performed live with such literary dignitaries as Raymond Federman, Pierre Joris, Andrew Schelling, Elizabeth Robinson, and Anne Waldman.

www.ingramcontent.com/pod-product-compliance
Lightning Source LLC
Chambersburg PA
CBHW022153080426
42734CB00006B/420